hygiene. She would also take food and warm clothes or blankets to them when these items were needed.

The attitude of whites toward blacks in the South was cordial but patronizing. There was much affection and little hostility. But there was also an absolute understanding that the two races did not mix socially, attend the same schools or churches, or—in most cases—even go to the same restaurants and businesses.

Jimmy's parents disagreed about blacks. Miss Lillian was very liberal and welcomed blacks into her home. But her husband was much more typical of Southerners of the time. If a black came to visit, Earl Carter quietly left the house.

Jimmy and Gloria flank their mother, Lillian.

9

Growing Up
in Georgia

Jimmy was the oldest of the four Carter children. When he was two, his sister Gloria was born. Three years later they were joined by sister Ruth. And finally, when Jimmy was 13, brother Billy came along.

When the Carter children were growing up, their house was without electricity, telephone, and heating. For most of Carter's childhood, the house had no running water. Not until Jimmy was 13 did the family have electricity. But that did not mean the family was poor. It was just the way people lived in the rural South some 70 year ago.

The Carters, in fact, were somewhat better off than most of their neighbors. The house was a big clapboard affair with two fireplaces. It was set in a grove of magnolia, nut, and fruit trees. After the house was wired for electricity, the family bought a radio, which put them in touch with the world beyond Plains. It was the only radio for miles around.

Earl Carter had a store in Plains where he sold feed and other supplies. Sometimes Mrs. Carter worked as a nurse. Until Jimmy Carter was 14, Miss Lillian cut his hair. The Carters always had an automobile. They were members of the Plains Baptist Church and attended services there regularly. Mr. Carter served as a deacon on the church board.

As a boy, Jimmy loved to hunt and fish. On the farm Jimmy grew up around animals—horses, pigs, and cows. He could ride a horse almost as early as he could remember.

Jimmy wore the number 10 on his Plains basketball team uniform.

He had particularly fond memories of a dog named Bozo and a horse called Lady Lee.

To make money for himself, young Jimmy picked, cleaned, roasted, and packed bags of peanuts. Then he carried them to town in his wagon and sold them for 5 cents a bag. By age 13, Carter had saved enough money to make a down payment on five houses which were rented out to town residents.

Young Jimmy liked to roam through the outdoors with his friends, many of whom were black. The boy also enjoyed sports and was a good student who took pleasure in reading. His favorite book was Tolstoy's *War and Peace.* Although the book was some 1,400 pages long, Jimmy loved the sweeping Russian historical novel about the Napoleonic period. But it wasn't just the battles that he found exciting. He was also eager to learn how war touched the lives of all kinds of people.

It was Miss Lillian who instilled in her family the love of reading. She taught Jimmy to read when he was four. In school he earned praise and gold stars on a special reading chart for students. The family even read at the dinner table. Meals could be interrupted, Miss Lillian believed, but reading time should not be.

On to Annapolis

Carter graduated from high school in 1941, when he was just 16. Jimmy wanted very much to go to the United States Naval Academy in Annapolis, Maryland, for his college training. The boy had dreamed of going there ever since he was 6 years old. His ambition dated from his early memories of his mother's brother, a naval officer.

But Jimmy had not yet secured the congressional appointment that was necessary to enroll in the academy. As class valedictorian, Carter had won a scholarship to Georgia Southwestern College. However, Jimmy turned over this scholarship to another student who would not have been able to afford to attend.

Carter when he graduated from Annapolis

Carter also felt he was too young and inexperienced, so he first spent a year at Georgia Southwestern College, a junior college. There he was able to supplement his meager knowledge of science and mathematics. These subjects had not been taught at Plains High School. He then spent another year at the Georgia Institute of Technology. By the time his appointment to the Naval Academy came through, Carter at last felt qualified to enroll at Annapolis.

At 18, Carter was ready for classes at the demanding naval school. Carter stood his full height of 5 feet 9 inches, and his weight was about 155 pounds. Because of World War II, the normal four-year course at Annapolis had been compressed into three. In 1943 Carter found life at the academy rough.

One of Jimmy Carter's strongest features was his toothy smile. But at Annapolis his fellow cadets thought he smiled too much. In order to satisfy the upperclassmen, one of the first things Carter had to do was to wipe the smile off his face.

Discipline was strict and the course work was tough. Annapolis students rose at 6:15 A.M. and had classes, drill, study, and work all day. The students were in bed, with lights out by 10 each night. Carter's extra schooling before coming to Annapolis paid off, though. He eventually earned an engineering degree.

Rosalynn Smith

In the summer of 1944, Jimmy met a young woman named Rosalynn Smith. He was nearly 20 and she was 17. Rosalynn had been born on August 18, 1927, also in Plains. Her father, Edgar Smith, was an auto mechanic. He died of leukemia, a blood disease, when Rosalynn was only 13.

While growing up, she later recalled, "We were very, very, very poor and we worked very hard." Rosalynn's mother was named Allie Murray Smith. Mrs. Smith supported her four children with a job at the local post office. She also took in sewing. As soon as she was old enough, Rosalynn pitched in to help. She took a job working in a beauty parlor in Plains.

Because Plains was such a small town, the Carters and the Smiths knew each other. The families became close when Miss Lillian helped Mrs. Smith nurse her husband through his final illness.

The happy couple on July 7, 1946

Although the families had known each other for years, the two young people had not really paid much attention to each other. But when Jimmy Carter and Rosalynn Smith finally became aware of each other, it was love at first sight. Carter has steadfastly said that there was never any other woman for him. They began writing to each other and seeing each other during breaks from school.

The match was a natural one. Both young people were hardworking and ambitious, eager to get ahead. Rosalynn Smith and Jimmy Carter were married on July 7, 1946, in the Methodist church in Plains. It was just one month after Carter graduated from Annapolis and had been commissioned as an ensign. Rosalynn had recently completed her work at a local junior college. World War II was over , and Carter was beginning a career as a naval officer on the rise.

The Navy Years

Carter embarked on an 8-year stint in the navy. During this time there were long periods when he and Rosalynn were apart. Rosalynn gave birth on July 3, 1947, to their first child—John William ("Jack"). When Carter was sent to Hawaii in December 1948, Rosalynn and the young child remained home. James Earl Carter III (or "Chip") was born April 12, 1950. Although she was basically a shy person, Rosalynn enjoyed the role of navy wife very much.

During much of this time, Carter traveled back and forth to various naval bases. He was in Portsmouth, Virginia, and Hawaii; twice he saw duty in New London, Connecticut.

In 1948 Carter applied to be part of the navy's nuclear submarine program. It was then regarded as one of the navy's most elite projects. Carter was interviewed—and hired—by Hyman Rickover, the tough-minded admiral who had created the nuclear program.

A third son, Donnel Jeffrey, was born to the Carters on August 18, 1952. In March of 1953 the Carters were sent to Schenectady, New York. During his time there, Carter studied at Union College, a small, prestigious school offering courses in engineering and liberal arts. The navy's nuclear submarine program was going full strength in Schenectady at facilities operated by the General Electric Company.

In the summer of 1953, Jimmy's father died from cancer at the age of 59. Jimmy was terribly shaken by his father's death. He decided to leave the navy. He, Rosalynn, and the boys returned to Plains around Christmas of 1953.

Jimmy had chosen to give up his naval career. Rosalynn was not happy about the move, and she struggled to accept the decision. Both Rosalynn and Jimmy had enjoyed their lives away from Georgia, and the prospect of returning to the small town made her uneasy. But she finally gave in. At his mother's urging, Jimmy took over running the family farm and other businesses.

Jimmy Carter set out to do what he knew best: peanut farming. But because the family's affairs were in disarray, Carter had to make some smart decisions. He took courses in finance and agriculture. More than anything, he wanted to make a success of the family business. Jimmy and his mother formed a partnership. Soon younger brother Billy joined in the venture. And, keeping things within the family, Rosalynn served as accountant for the firm. Within ten years the business was making more than $1 million a year.

Jimmy became a well-known figure in Plains. He served as scoutmaster for his sons' Boy Scout troops. He also became a deacon on the board of the Plains Baptist Church, just as his father had been. Carter had always believed that blacks and whites should have equal opportunities. Not many other Southerners agreed with him in the mid-1950s. But then a dispute over the desegregation laws of 1954 forced him to resign from his position on the board of the church.

Jimmy Carter in 1966

Jimmy "Who?"

Jimmy entered politics slowly. He began by becoming involved in local politics. He took a great interest in his children's schooling and became a member of the local school board.

Then in September 1962 Carter decided to run for a state senate seat. Carter won, but only after a close race. There was evidence of election fraud. Ballot boxes had been illegally stuffed by Carter's opponent. Carter insisted upon a recount, and the new results enabled him to claim his senate seat. Once he became a senator, he was able to achieve reforms that were needed in local politics.

Beginning in January 1963, Carter worked out of Atlanta's state capitol building. He remained a state senator for four years. During a period when many white Georgians were still opposed to integration, Carter took a positive stand in favor of desegregation.

In March of 1966, Carter began a campaign to run for U.S. senator. But one of his rivals dropped out of the race to run for governor of Georgia. And Carter—unwisely, as it turned out—made the same switch. They were both up against the colorful but racist incumbent, Lester Maddox.

Carter miscalculated. Although he, Rosalynn, and the children campaigned strenuously, they did not have a significant impact. They personally met and spoke to some 300,000 people, but almost no one had any real idea of who this man was. In fact, "Jimmy Who?" became his nickname. When the votes were counted, Jimmy came in a pitiful third.

Although he had been defeated, Jimmy Carter was not a sore loser. He would try to run for governor again in 1970. What would he do for four long years? He decided, quite simply, that he would learn everything there was to know about running for governor—and winning. If it took four years to do this, then so be it.

Once again Carter and his family went out to the people. He continued to serve on the boards of charities and other worthy causes. In short order Jimmy Carter had become one of the most influential people in southwest Georgia. In the midst of the preparations, Rosalynn gave birth to the Carters' fourth child and only daughter. Amy Lynn Carter was born on October 19, 1967.

On the campaign trail, the Carters met a lot of people. This time the estimate was closer to 600,000. Carter made almost 2,000 speeches in an effort to win over the voters. No longer would he be known as "Jimmy Who?"

The hard work did in fact pay off. In the primary in September 1970, Carter defeated his Democratic rival. And in the general election some weeks later, he beat the Republican candidate. On January 12, 1971, Carter was sworn in as governor of Georgia.

First Stop: Governor

Carter turned out to be a strong governor of Georgia. Under his leadership blacks were given many fresh opportunities. The number of blacks in government jobs grew by 30 percent while Carter was in office. Georgia's state government had hundreds of overlapping agencies, many of whose employees performed exactly the same tasks. Carter formulated the Agency Reform Act, which once and for all clarified agency functions and eliminated overlap and waste.

Ever the populist, Carter set up many community centers as well. Rosalynn, too, was suddenly thrust into the limelight. Life in the public eye was quite a shift for her and her children.

Success went to Carter's head. Many of his advisers strongly recommended that Carter consider running for president. But all plans were kept secret. A president needs to know a great deal about foreign countries and their policies. Carter didn't, but he used every possible opportunity to learn about other world powers.

In 1973 Governor Carter was appointed co-chair of the Democratic party's 1974 campaign committee. He was in a position to tap into the talents of many well-known Democrats. The job put him in an ideal spot to learn what he could about the internal workings of the party and, on a larger scale, government as a whole. And Carter made use of every opportunity. In fact, he spent a great deal of this time positioning himself for his own campaign.

On December 12, 1974, Carter announced officially that he would seek the presidency in 1976. Since Rosalynn had spearheaded Carter's early campaigns for the Georgia senate seat and then for the governorship, it was no surprise that she was instrumental in helping Jimmy decide that he would run for president.

Carter's mother was not always as supportive. When her son told her of his decision to run for president, Miss Lillian's reaction was: "President of what?"

Despite the fact that Carter was a political unknown in the nation and had had limited experience in government, he won his party's nomination for president. His ambition, sense of purpose, and energetic campaigning in the primaries helped him defeat his rivals. Carter accepted his party's nomination in July 1976 at the Democratic convention in New York City. Carter then chose Walter F. Mondale, a senator from Minnesota, as his vice presidential running mate.

Yet again the Carter family banded together and campaigned, this time for the nation's highest office. Carter visited some 43 states, many of them with Rosalynn and at least a few of them with some of the children. Rosalynn kept herself well informed and was able to speak effectively with reporters and journalists about important issues and their significance.

In July of 1976 Carter won the Democratic party nomination for president. Surrounding him: Mother Lillian, daughter Amy, son Jack, Rosalynn, son Jeff and Jeff's wife, Annette, and son Chip.

During the presidential campaign of 1976, Carter had only a little time for relaxation. Here he chats in Plains with daughter Amy and his mother, Miss Lillian.

Rosalynn proved to be a tireless campaigner, regularly putting in 16-hour days five days a week. In the mornings—often as early as 4 A.M.—she would show up to talk with factory workers. Afternoons were spent addressing religious groups and women's groups. In the evenings she would attend dinners, rallies, and press conferences. Rosalynn campaigned for her husband in 96 cities in 36 states.

In despair at not being elected governor of Georgia in 1966, Carter had turned to religion. He communed with his sister, Ruth Carter Stapleton, a Baptist evangelist. He became a born-again Christian. Would Carter's newfound Christian zeal be a help or a hindrance to becoming president? There were some people who felt that Carter would not be able to keep church and state separate, as the Constitution requires. But there were other voters for whom Carter's strong faith was a positive factor rather than a problem.

Carter was running against President Gerald Ford. Ford had become vice president first and then president in a set of bizarre circumstances never before encountered in American history. Spiro Agnew had been Richard Nixon's vice president. But in the face of scandal, Agnew was forced to resign in 1973. Ford was named vice president to replace Agnew. Then in 1974 Richard Nixon himself chose to resign under the threat of impeachment. In this way Ford had become the first president in the 200-year history of the United States to be chosen rather than elected either as president or as vice president.

Ford had proven to be a lackluster, caretaker-type of president. With Ford's uninspiring performance, following several years of scandal under Agnew and Nixon, it is not surprising that the country was looking for new leadership. The 1976 presidential race between Ford and Carter was a close one, however. The popular vote went to Carter, with 50.1 percent, and Ford gathered 48 percent. Carter received 297 electoral votes while Ford garnered 24.

Tears of delight unite Jimmy and Rosalynn at the announcement that Carter has been elected president.

Carter in Office

Carter was a strong individual with high moral principles. He refused to be labeled either as a liberal or as a conservative. And in many ways he was right. In some senses he was both, and in other ways he did not fit into either of these convenient political categories.

When Carter came to office, the country was beset by a cluster of persistent economic problems. Unemployment was widespread, and inflation continued at a galloping pace. In Carter's second year as president, inflation climbed to more than 10 percent, a record in American history. The steep rise in the cost of goods and services led to a new expression, "double-digit" inflation. It didn't matter, somehow, that unemployment figures had dropped. Although many new jobs had been created by the Carter administration, Americans seemed to notice only the inflation figures.

25

In 1977, political conditions in many of the oil-producing countries caused fuel shortages in nations that imported crude oil for processing in their refineries. Carter asked Americans to unite to help overcome the shortages. Conservation measures had been used during wartime but never before when the United States was at peace. Now it was suggested that energy cutbacks might be the way of the future.

In the early months of 1979 a revolution took place in Iran, one of the world's major oil-producing countries. Iran's shah—to whom the American government had been friendly—had been deposed. Along with the shah went most of Iran's stability. As a result, much of the Middle East's oil was kept away from the United States, and the gasoline shortage became even more acute. Many service stations had limited supplies, and in some places gas was even rationed. By the summer the situation was dire.

As a result, Carter pressed, throughout his presidency, for energy-saving measures and programs. He ran up against many political obstacles, including special-interest groups. Among them was the oil industry, which was making huge profits in the midst of the oil squeeze. It was not until the spring of 1980 that Carter's new energy program was passed by the Senate. His energy legislation was among the most important of all Carter's domestic plans.

Not surprisingly, the energy crisis did not help Carter's popularity. The president did what he had to do. He lectured the nation on the need to conserve, asking for a commitment to reducing waste that he called the "moral equivalent of war."

Carter also wanted to reorganize many of the federal government's agencies. As he had found in Georgia, many agencies were overlapping and doing the same work as others.

Carter suffered some embarrassment when two of his top appointees were forced to leave office. Bert Lance, the budget director, was found guilty of some shady financial dealings in his private life and willingly resigned. And Carter's appointee as ambassador to the United Nations proved to be a liability. Andrew Young said too many of the wrong things at the wrong time, and was removed from his post.

As first lady, Rosalynn Carter commanded her own staff of 18. All first ladies are expected to take an active role in social programs. Rosalynn's particular interests included work on behalf of mental health programs, the needs of the elderly, and the Equal Rights Amendment to the Constitution. The ERA, which would have guaranteed equal rights for women, was not ratified.

In 1977 Rosalynn was sent on her own tour of seven Latin American and Caribbean countries. Her function was to serve as the president's representative. She met with government leaders and held important policy discussions with them. It was a very responsible role for a first lady.

Negotiations Overseas

Delicate negotiations continued with the Soviet Union, the United States' only serious rival. The strategic arms limitation talks in Vienna in 1970 had produced the SALT I treaty. Because the pact was in need of serious revision, SALT II went to the top of Carter's agenda. The president's intent was to cut back nuclear weapons and thus reduce the possibility of large-scale war. It seemed that both superpowers really wanted the agreement, but the diplomatic dance surrounding the treaty was a nervous time. Carter and Soviet leader Leonid Brezhnev met several times.

Finally, in June 1979, the SALT II treaty was signed. Now Carter had to get the Senate to go along with the terms of the pact. It was almost ready to do this, but just after Christmas 1979, the Soviets invaded the country of Afghanistan. All the steps forward toward U.S.-Soviet détente—the lessening of tensions between the two superpowers—were now reversed. And so Carter suffered another major disappointment.

— Under Carter, diplomatic relations were established with Communist-controlled China. For years the only Chinese government that was recognized by the United States was the one on the island of Taiwan. Now, mainland China, and its capital of Beijing, were being acknowledged by the U.S. government.

Another foreign policy issue facing the Carter presidency was the fate of the Panama Canal. When the waterway was built in 1914, Panama gave away most of its control of the Canal Zone to the United States. Many people felt that the Panama Canal and the Canal Zone should be returned to Panama. Some, including Ronald Reagan, thought that America was giving away territory unnecessarily. Finally, in 1978, two treaties were ratified by the Senate. The agreements stated that most of the land would be returned to Panama in 1999 and also gave the United States the right to defend the land.

Carter's hopes for the United States were thwarted by spiraling inflation, mounting energy costs, and the continuing threat of communism. Although Carter's foreign policy program was beset by difficulties from the start, it did see some achievements.

Carter spent many hours during his term dealing with the sensitive global issue of human rights. In many countries, people's rights were being ignored and in some cases brutally violated. On occasion, the United States threatened to withhold either financial support or trade agreements from nations with poor human rights records. Carter hoped this would force other countries to reevaluate their positions.

Middle East Troubles

Carter was able to bring Egypt and Israel together for peace talks in 1978. In September of that year Carter hosted a meeting between President Anwar Sadat of Egypt and the prime minister of Israel, Menachem Begin. The idea was to secure peace in the Middle East. For 13 days the three leaders met at Camp David, the presidential retreat about 90 miles from Washington.

Deep-seated animosities between Egypt and Israel caused many tense moments in the negotiations. On at least two occasions Sadat threatened to pack his bags and return home. At one point Sadat and Begin refused to speak to each other directly. Carter was left to mediate, through interpreters, between the two of them.

But finally, on September 17, the two representatives signed a "framework" agreement. The result was a treaty known as the Camp David accord. On March 26 of the following year, the peace treaty was actually signed—on the south lawn of the White House.

Carter applauds as Egypt's Anwar Sadat and Israel's Menachem Begin embrace in the East Room of the White House. Agreements for peace in the Middle East had just been signed.

Carter's biggest headache came with the continuing problems in Iran. In January 1979 the shah of Iran had fled his country. His moderate policies had brought Iran immense prosperity. But many Iranians thought he was a dictator, and he was an unpopular figure. He wanted to emigrate to the United States, but Carter saw this as a dangerous step. Instead the shah want to Egypt and other nations.

Soon after the shah left Iran, he was replaced by the Ayatollah Khomeini, long in exile in France. Unlike the shah, Khomeini was a religious fanatic.

Then it was discovered that the deposed shah was seriously ill with cancer, and he came to the United States for treatment in October 1979. This enraged many Iranians, and Iranians around the world demonstrated against the United States. In November, protesters in front of the American embassy in Iran's capital, Tehran, stormed the building and held all the inhabitants prisoners. A few of the hostages were quickly released, but 52 remained in captivity, innocent political prisoners.

Carter watched all these events with deep concern. He was so distressed by these flagrant violations of human rights that for the first time in many years there was no lighted Christmas tree on the White House lawn. The president had decided to dispense with this sign of holiday celebration as a tribute to the American prisoners being held hostage.

A special rescue team was sent out in April 1980 to storm the embassy and set the hostages free. But through a series of bungles and mishaps, the rescue plan was a disas-

A failed rescue attempt at freeing the hostages held in Iran turned out to be a bad step in Carter's presidency.

trous failure. Eight lives were lost when a helicopter and a plane—both part of the rescue team—collided. A second rescue plan was formed, but the Iranians learned of it in advance and moved the hostages to different locations.

While all this was going on, Carter was trying to run for reelection as president. He was up against the very popular Ronald Reagan, former Republican governor of California. The hostage crisis was just one of the things that prevented Jimmy Carter from winning a second term. Another liability was brother Billy. He had a drinking problem and went around the world making inappropriate remarks. But Reagan's immense popularity was the primary reason for Carter's defeat.

All of Carter's achievements in foreign policy were overshadowed by the continuing hostage crisis in Iran. Oddly enough, Carter's indefatigable efforts to secure the hostages' release from the embassy in Iran actually did result in their return to freedom. But Carter was never able to reap the reward of his coup, since Reagan was about to replace him as president of the United States.

On Election Day in 1980, Carter was trounced by Reagan, both in the electoral college vote and in the popular vote. The final insult came on Reagan's inauguration day, January 20, 1981. On that day, the hostages were freed and on their way back to America. By then it was too late for Carter. Ronald Reagan was left to bask in the glory.

The happiness was short-lived on Election Day 1980.

The Carter
White House

President Carter rose at 6:30 each morning. Sometimes, if the weather was chilly, he would light a fire in one of the White House fireplaces. After a cup of coffee and a quick look at the morning's newspapers, his public day would begin. By 8 A.M. he was meeting with cabinet members or other government leaders. At least one day a week Carter reserved for lunch alone with Rosalynn.

Rosalynn was an independent first lady. She headed a drive to look after America's mentally ill. Because of her position as Jimmy's closest adviser, Rosalynn often found herself challenged by detractors. Some even called her co-president. But no first lady was ever better prepared to assume this role. Rosalynn Carter was recognized by her husband as a political equal. She even attended cabinet meetings.

But Mrs. Carter was also a gracious hostess who brought an atmosphere of informality to the White House and its private living quarters. Like many recent first ladies, Rosalynn thought the solarium at the top of the White House made a perfect family room, and the Carters spent many happy hours there. The Carters fitted out another family sitting room with barnwood paneling from their Georgia farm. A close couple, the Carters shared a bed-room. Rosalynn and Jimmy took turns each night reading passages from the Bible before turning in.

Carter drew on the popularity of earlier Democratic presidents. He sat at the same desk John F. Kennedy had used in the Oval Office. It was the one fashioned from the timbers of the ship *Resolute.* The desk had been a gift from England's Queen Victoria to President Rutherford B. Hayes.

Carter broke White House tradition in several ways. Miss Lillian, Carter's mother, was given some official duties. She was even sent abroad as the president's representative to important meetings and on official visits. The wizened, white-haired woman was a forthright figure. She became a colorful and well-liked fixture during the Carter years in office. She was nicknamed "first mother" by members of the press.

Carter's mother was a popular figure during her son's presidency.

In 1966, at 68, Miss Lillian had joined the Peace Corps. She went to India and worked there for two years as a nurse. Most people admired her independence and spirit. And for many older Americans she stood as a role model for an active and involved life-style.

The Carters entertained, but in a much homier style than almost any of their recent predecessors. On one occasion, however, the Carters did entertain lavishly. When the Camp David peace accord was signed in 1979, the Carters threw a dinner for 1,300 guests. With almost no advance warning, the White House chef and staff produced a festive meal served in tents on the White House lawn.

In 1979 the Carters welcomed Pope John Paul II to the White House. At that time he had been pontiff for only one year. John Paul was the first pope to meet with a president in the executive mansion.

Even as president, Jimmy Carter remained an avid reader. In addition to the papers and documents that were part of his job, he still read three or four books each week. A speed reader, Carter was able to take in 2,000 words a minute, and could remember 95 percent of what he read.

First Daughter

Amy Carter was nine when the Carters came to the White House in 1977. It had been several years since the preteen child of a president had grown up in the White House. The Kennedy children had been little more than infants, and the Johnson and Nixon daughters, as well as the Fords' youngest children, were almost grown-ups when they came to live there.

The Carters hired a nursemaid for Amy. The nation watched Amy's adolescence unfold in newspaper articles and on television. Each day when Amy left to go to school, a Secret Service agent accompanied her. And the agent sat through Amy's classes with her.

Amy Carter was one of the youngest children to grow up in the White House. Here she and her parents board a helicopter to fly to Camp David.

When the Carters moved in to the White House, Amy brought with her a seal point Siamese cat named Misty Malarkey Ying Yang. Then her fourth grade teacher presented her with a spotted, mixed breed puppy the family immediately christened Grits. But Grits did not remain a member of the household for long.

Grits proved to be a dog with ideas of his own. He refused to cooperate with a veterinarian who wanted to test the dog for heartworm in front of live television cameras during an animal health care promotion. And Grits did not get along with his White House mate, the Carter cat. It was not long before the Carters sent Grits back to Amy's teacher.

Amy celebrated her tenth birthday on October 19, 1977, while the Carters were in the White House. The theme was a Halloween party, and Amy and her schoolmates were treated to darkened rooms and spooky noises. The youngsters also watched the original *Frankenstein* movie, starring Boris Karloff.

Young Amy used the White House bowling alley on many occasions. And President Carter, still trim and fit, kept himself so with frequent games of tennis on the White House courts. The Carters all enjoyed the White House indoor swimming pool.

After the White House

Unlike many first families leaving the White House, the Carters did not return to private life as happy people. Both Rosalynn and Jimmy were bitterly disappointed with American voters. They could not understand how the nation had turned against Jimmy so strongly.

As soon as Jimmy Carter was out of the White House, he flew to Germany to meet with the freed American hostages. Wiesbaden, near Frankfurt, was a halfway stopping-off place for the hostages. There he met them all and convinced them of the work he had done in their behalf.

Billy Carter's mismanagement of the peanut business had cost the family a lot of money. Carter's first job in Plains was to get the once-successful business back on its feet. Then Jimmy began to teach courses in government at Emory University in Atlanta.

In retirement the Carters have lectured and written. They have lived quietly in Plains, Georgia, maintaining their interests and running the family business. Together the Carters have worked on behalf of social causes—especially housing for low-income families and the homeless.

In retirement the Carters helped out on housing projects.

For many Americans it was particularly gratifying during the 1980s to see both Carters on their hands and knees helping out at inner-city housing projects.

While Carter was president, Plains enjoyed a brief period of fame and prosperity. Property values sky-rocketed, and curiosity seekers flocked there to see the president's hometown. Perhaps visitors could even pick up a piece of Carter memorabilia. On most weekends, tourists outnumbered town residents two to one. After the Carters left the White House, the town returned to its sleepy simplicity.

Both Jimmy and Rosalynn wrote their own books. Jimmy Carter's memoirs were called *Keeping Faith*. They were published in 1982. Rosalynn's book, published in 1984, was called *First Lady from Plains*. Together the former first couple coauthored *Everything to Gain: Making the Most of the Rest of Your Life*. This book told of the Carters' lives together since leaving the White House.

Rosalynn has not been entirely satisfied with the return to the quiet life in Plains. She has even toyed with the idea of running for political office. She has not ruled out the possibility of serving in the Senate or the House of Representatives.

When Jimmy Carter left the White House, he was not yet 60 years old. Even as he approaches 70, Carter is still youthful and fit. He enjoys working in his wood shop, where he crafts handmade furniture.

The Reagans and the Carters at the 1986 opening of the Jimmy Carter Library in Atlanta, Georgia.

The Carters have cherished the opportunity to spend time at home visiting with their children and grand-children. All three Carter sons have gone into business—not politics. And, once out of the public eye, Amy Carter tried to pursue normal studies. She has turned up on a few occasions herself, protesting some of the more unpopular measures of her father's presidential successors. The spunky Miss Lillian died of cancer in 1983 at the age of 85.

Both Jimmy and Rosalynn Carter were conspicuous at President Bill Clinton's inaugural ceremony in January 1993. Clinton is also a Southerner as well as a fellow Democrat. Clinton may see in the Carters an image of the timeless values of the South—the devotion to home, family, honor, and simplicity—that he wants to be hallmarks of his own presidency.

The James Earl Carter Library is located in Americus, Georgia, on the campus of Georgia Southwestern College. The school is one of Jimmy's Carter's alma maters. The Carter Library is a study center holding many of the president's papers, photos, and family memorabilia. In addition, the Carter Presidential Center was established in Atlanta, Georgia. This library is devoted to documents relating to Carter's years as president.

The Carter Legacy

Jimmy Carter was one of our most enigmatic presidents. He showed the value of hard work and demonstrated that persistence can pay off. He also showed innate intelligence: a mistake once made would never be made a second time. He was a member of the "new South." He respected age-old traditions, but he also saw the South as a place where new attitudes were forming and growing. Some of the nation's fastest-growing cities were in the South, and the area was becoming one of increasing prosperity and political power.

Jimmy Carter was a knowledgeable and well-read president. Perhaps his views were too one-dimensional and simplistic. Some people described him as stubborn and strong willed. The same people also said that Carter had a deep-seated belief that he was never wrong. However much Carter hated to make mistakes or admit to having made them, though, he did accept full blame for the military disaster of the botched hostage rescue effort.

Carter's honesty was also one of his strong points. A sense of belonging, a sense of family, was another. The Carter family heritage was a major aspect of Jimmy's character. Family history was important to him. He thought that Americans should get to know their family tree: who their ancestors and relatives were, where they came from, and where they are buried. Carter believed that such knowledge "would make a lot of difference in the way people think about themselves and other people around them." It would lead to a rebirth of individual pride, and love of country as well.

Carter was an engaging figure, a naval officer and businessman turned politician. He was a traditional Southerner, who at the same time tried to break with tradition. He was a devout Christian who tried to put his faith and principles to work for the country's good. As a result, he was perceived by some as weak and ineffective. But even Carter's detractors and worst enemies could find no trace of dishonesty and few personal faults in the man.

Carter's administration came at a difficult time. The country was still coming to terms with the aftermath of Vietnam as well as with the scandals of the Nixon years. A tough set of problems both at home and abroad confronted a president who genuinely strove to do his best for the country. Against this backdrop it is difficult to fairly and fully assess Carter's achievements.

Five U.S. presidents gathered in 1991: Bush, Reagan, Carter, Ford, and Nixon.

For Further Reading

Anthony, Carl Sferrazza. *First Ladies: The Saga of the Presidents' Wives and Their Power, 1961-1990*. New York: William Morrow and Company, 1991.

Fisher, Leonard Everett. *The White House*. New York: Holiday House, 1989.

Friedel, Frank. *The Presidents of the United States of America*. Revised edition. Washington, D.C.: The White House Historical Association, 1989.

Klapthor, Margaret Brown. *The First Ladies*. Revised edition. Washington, D.C.: The White House Historical Association, 1989.

Lindsay, Rae. *The Presidents' First Ladies*. New York: Franklin Watts, 1989.

The Living White House. Revised edition. Washington, D.C.: The White House Historical Association, 1987.

Poynter, Margaret. *The Jimmy Carter Story*. New York: Julian Messner, 1978.

Richman, Daniel A. *James E. Carter, 39th President of the United States*. Ada, Oklahoma: Garrett Educational Corporation, 1989.

St. George, Judith. *The White House: Cornerstone of a Nation*. New York: G. P. Putnam's Sons, 1990.

Smith , Betsy Covington. *Jimmy Carter, President*. New York: Walker and Company, 1986.

Wade, Linda R. *James Carter*. Chicago: Childrens Press, 1989.

Index